Resurrecting The Pierced Heart

It is a Journey with an Amazing Reward

Sherri C Rouse

Cover Design by Sherri C Rouse

I dedicate this book first and foremost to my Lord and Savior, whose love never fails. It is also dedicated to Rick and Sherry Schenck for their encouragement and for being an amazing part of my healing. Thank you both for the many hours you spent editing and just working with me.

Romans 8:18 (NIV)
I consider that our present sufferings are not worth comparing with the glory that will be revealed in us.

Table of Contents

Author

Sherri C Rouse, a native of North Carolina, was born in Rocky Mount and raised in an orphanage for fourteen and a half years. I am the proud mother of two beautiful women and three grandchildren. In my free time, I love being with my grandchildren and doing fun activities with them. Writing poems is such a joy and relaxing outlet that allows me to glorify God. This collection of poems includes spiritual writings, appreciation for special friends and tributes to those who influenced my life. This collection was inspired by the Trinity (Father, Son, and Holy Spirit). Earlier poems were born of feelings and my personal history before God transformed my heart. He has been bringing me back to His original design, to which I am eternally grateful. I love the way that He continues to heal and grow me into His beautiful butterfly that I have always been, but unable to recognize.

Preface

This book is a collection of God inspired poems I have written over many years. Most were from my life experiences, some were from people that I have met along my journey, and a few were written for a specific person or group of people. For example, "I Am Alive" was from a God given vision from the perspective of an unborn infant.

My prayer is that this poetry will help you realize that the Father loves you and can transform your heart. No matter the amount of hurt or piercing, He can heal and refashion it. The Father's love can bring you through anything. Genuine joy and peace can be yours. Even though struggles will come, He can use them to reshape you and make you whole. I pray that these poems show you that the loving Holy Spirit can lead you out of the valley with a completely transformed heart, full of dependence on God.

His love never fails!

CHAPTER 1
DARKNESS
(BEFORE SURRENDERING TO CHRIST)

Screeching Pain

Screeching pain inside and out
Continuously I feel your hands ripping me apart
Your feet trample over me day and night
The walls inside me slowly bleeding
Moment by moment
"Please!", I cry," End this pain!"
Break the rope, let me go
Screeching pain, let me die

Look at me, see the hurt
Feel the shaking of my hands in fear
Of the next pain you will push on me
Look inside of me; darkness lingers with tears that bleed
The pain you shove on me is screeching over me
You see my tears and beg for more
Never once did I ask for this, so Please,
"End this screeching pain"

Your words of hate and ugliness playing
Over and over in my mind
Please look inside me and see my heart
Bleeding, broken in many pieces
Why can't you see?
Please feel this pain overtaking me
The pain screeching, crawling like worms
All inside and out of me

All I ask is to end this screeching pain;

Instead, I receive even more pain and black roses
The petals fall one by one
My tears bleed
As the pain covers me
You killed my past and my present,
And I see no future
Please end this screeching pain that bleeds on me

Imagine

Close your eyes and imagine
A little blue eyed boy being thrown against a wall
Look deep within
See a little brown haired girl being held upside down and
Beat
Close your eyes and imagine
A small child being dragged by the hair across the rocks
Can you feel the pain?
Imagine being forced to eat or feel a broomstick
Across your back
Imagine a small brown-eyed blonde haired little
Girl locked in a closet…
Being stomped and thrown around
Close your eyes and imagine all the pain and fear
Ha, I don't need to imagine for I felt it all in your "care"

What You Gave me

You gave me food...for what?

To feed the pain you gave me!

You gave me clothes...for what?

To cover the scars you gave me!

You gave me a bed...for what?

To lay down my broken self!

Oh yes, you gave me an education...for what?

To make yourselves look good!

You even gave me a roof over my head...for what?

To hide your constant abuse!

Why didn't you give me a bucket for

All the tears you gave me?

Ha, there is something missing here…

Love you never gave!

In Your Little Closet

In your little closet you lock me away
I sit shivering in fear wondering when you will return
Holding back the tears for fear you might see or hear me cry
It’s so scary and dark in your little closet
Please...Please someone please come rescue me
Yes! Finally I hear footsteps and laughter
The door opens to your little closet
Smiling and laughing as you look at me
Sorry little one I forgot you
Oh how I have to fight to hold the tears
For fear you will see me cry
I know you will lock me in your closet if I cry
Laugh...laugh you continue on with your laugh

Does It Matter

We may be young and small but we feel,
Does it matter?
How you hit us
What you throw at us
Does it matter?
The ugly names
The beatings you all give
All the abuse
Does it matter?
I often wonder
As I lay and wait for the next attack
Young or small why
Doesn't it matter?
Please don't hurt us any more!

Darkness

Darkness all around
I open my eyes and the darkness is always there
I close my eyes and just more darkness
Darkness… Nothing but a hole full of emptiness
So many emotions and feelings stirring in the dark
More darkness comes with all the feelings and emotions
Stirring
You took away everything from me and left nothing
Nothing but darkness and terror
Why did you leave me this way?

Your hands bring pain
Your hands made my eyes to see nothing but darkness
Darkness in every corner with the sound of terror
The face you see is my own completely full
Of darkness where terror roams
When darkness began to fall on me
All joy and confidence disappeared
When I think or feel the pain,and all you stole from me
Terror surrounds me inside and out

I fight to see a glimpse of light against all the pain inside me
Fear continues to creep in with each lonely thought
Inside me as darkness continues to fill me
Pain and fear I try to push on you just to let you feel
A little of the terror of Hell you put me through
Wishing I could give you back the darkness and then
Once again I could see the rainbow in the sky

No One

No one listens to the cries of a child

No one answers the why

A child exposed to ridicule, neglect, rejection,

Hate, violence, and sexual abuse

Why does this please all of you?

A father walks away

A mother looks away

No one fights to keep us together

No one cares

All are pleased, but me

You look at me with eyes of shame

You cut me with your lies

I scream in pain

No one answers my cries

No one answers my whys

Please heed the cries of a child!

Please No More

Oh, how one wishes to feel no more of your evil, but survive
We must,
As we remain in this place you all call a home
The pain is so devastating!
Most of you just enjoy bullying and tormenting moment by
Moment
Can't you see or feel the pain you are causing?
No! You enjoy the tears, the screaming, the feeling
Of satisfaction you get from teasing and hurting
You abuse power as an idol with no care at all
So long as you feel satisfaction,
And keep others under your power
You hold many under captivity with no escape
Except to hide within themselves
If you even cared for a moment, you would look and see
The bleeding inside and out
See and hear the many cries, but wait you do, and you crave
For more
Why do you continue to stab even more?
Ripping all to pieces like we're just trash, the same as you
Feed us
Well, I guess we are just children that don't matter,
For all you want is to feel the energetic, lightning power, and
Thrill of Blood rushing through you
You have no care that we are children wishing to be loved
Our tears mean nothing to a single one of you
All we want is to feel hands that touch without pain
Please no more!

Your hands and heart of evil one day will be destroyed by the

Giant that is coming to save the children and destroy your
Cult
Sacrifice no more, for the blood you use lacks all power
Please! We say NO MORE!

Mother Dear

Mother dear please accept me as I am

Wrap your arms around me

Even for a moment

Please, Let me feel you close to

Me for a few moments

Mother dear, I love you

Please, love me

Could you give me one hug?

Let me feel your love even for a moment

All I want mother dear is

To know you truly love me

Hold me close

Let me feel your heartbeat

Oh, how I wish to know

My mother's love

Even for a moment

CHAPTER 2
(FINDING TRUTH WHILE TRANSITIONING)

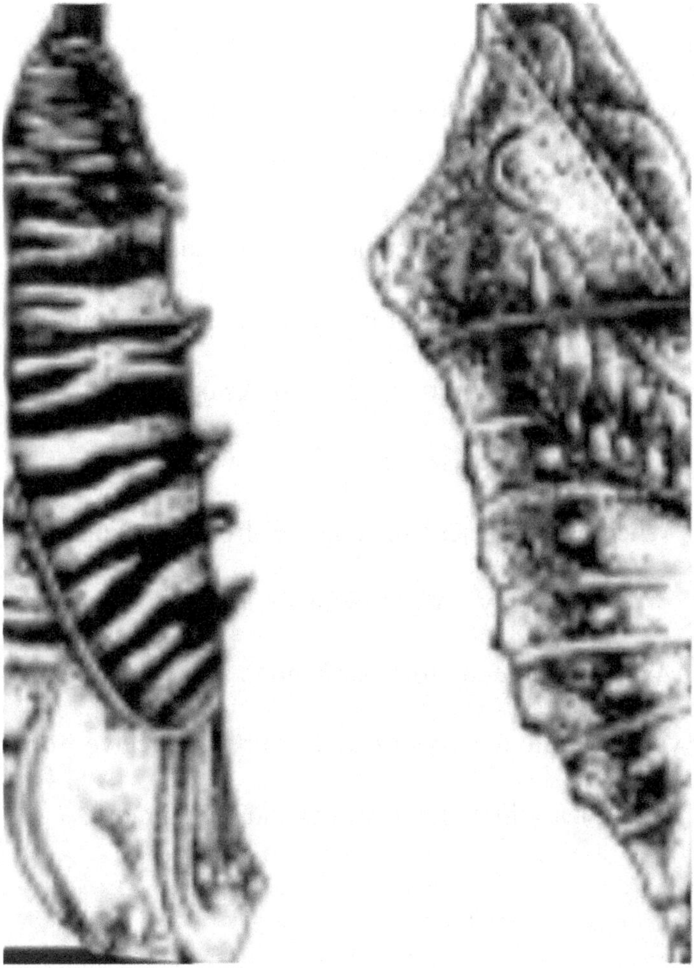

Eyes

My eyes lead you to my soul

Through my eyes you see all

As we look into each other's eyes, so many feelings stir

Within me

Oh, such anger and heartache I bring to you

The look of rejection for me is clearly seen in your eyes

I see you boiling ready to strike once again

You see, our eyes show all

There is a pain seen in your eyes from knowing me

Why do my eyes continue to draw you near?

Watching intently for your hand to strike once again

As you look into my eyes I feel the hurt you receive from me

Please look into my eyes and see no more

New Eyes

Thank you father for the new eyes
Eyes to see now the truth
Through the new eyes I see the true Father
I see the One who wipes away every tear and mends every
Heart
Through the new eyes I can see the little sparrow looking
Down at me
I now see and feel a mother's love that was unknown to me
My new eyes are now Your eyes
Now, through these new eyes, I see compassion
For those who hurt me
I see and feel compassion for those who don't see You

With my new eyes I see You Jesus the greatest gift of all
I now see Your beauty Your shining light
Mesmerized by the beauty of Your face
Through my new eyes I see and feel my heart change for You
I now see the purpose You have for me
With new eyes I now see love
I can love because you first loved me

Through these new eyes, You show me the beauty in me
You show me the beauty in others even though they don't see
You
Now, I see the suffering You did for me
I see through Your eyes how much You love us all
Through these new eyes I see the healing that came
From You dying
For my transgressions and iniquities

I see now that through my new eyes I am healed by Your Stripes

Now, through my new eyes You also live, for others see You In me

Thankful for new eyes

Who am I

I often wonder who I am

I am somebody, but who am I?

Days come, and days go,

And I just wonder, who am I?

I hide behind a mask,

So no one knows who I am

A mask full of pain and tears,

Broken in so many parts

Each part hides behind its own little mask,

Searching for a way to discover,

Who am I?

Please

Help me remove the mask and accept me

Just tell me who I am!

Who I Am

I no longer ask who I am,
For I know who I am
I am the Father's Creation!

I declare and affirm who I am...
I am a child of God, the giver of my daily bread
I am somebody;
Loved by my Creator

I am victorious
For through Christ,
I am more than a conqueror
I am a champion!
I am more than a survivor,
I am no longer a victim

Your words and hands of evil no longer hold me,
For my Abba Father forgives my debts,
And I forgive my debtors
Now, mended by the hands of love,
I am free...a champion
I know who I am

Yes, I am the righteousness of God through Jesus Christ
My Lord, saved by His grace,
Loved and gifted beyond measure
I know who I am because of the Creator,
Who created me in His image

I am His child, brilliantly and wonderfully made,

Willing to endure and to serve my Father
For my reward is a greater gift;
I am His chosen lovely rose forever

I am priceless and precious to my Savior
Who made me whole
I am cleansed by the Blood of the Lamb
I am wrapped in the Father's Hands
I am a beautiful treasure,
A chosen radiant pearl
I am priceless, I am loved, I am accepted
I know who I am!

I am who I am,
Defined by Father, Son and Spirit of Truth
I stand on Truth
I know who I am!

I am overrunning with joy,
For I know
Of His abundance for me
I am my Father's creation

I am full of wisdom and understanding
Every enemy will flee from me for
The Holy Spirit lives in me
I am beautiful, inside and out
I love me!

I know who I am!

Free Inside Me

Deep inside me I am free
You can't reach me
I am covered deep inside
For deep inside I am free
You can't see me
I can't feel the pain of your hands
Deep inside me free I am
You come to give me pain…
But I go deep inside to be Free

Safe, deep inside me, I can cry
Safe inside me, I can feel
I can let go freely without fear
Safe inside, I don't have to hide
I can scream, yell, or cry safe inside me
Safe inside, I am free to be me
Freely I can let the pain out deep inside
You will never know I set it free safe inside me
Free to be me, happy, sad, or mad
Safe inside I am free indeed

Secret Place

My secret place no darkness can touch
I hear your whispers as soft as the little sparrows voice
In this secret place all alone with you Lord,
I feel you holding me so intimately
Even with the trials that come upon me,
I can lay them down so easily in my secret place
Right at Your Feet
How lovely it is to lay safely in Your Arms,
And feel Your Peace so strongly
Oh how amazing to feel all my tears wiped away,
In my special secret place where I lie down,
All my thoughts and cares
Here in this special place, I feel the greatest
Joy and happiness I've ever known
My secret place where all dreams are seen
The place where You my Father truly extinguish the flames
And clear the smoke as I pour my heart and mind and soul
Out to you
The place I feel Your intimate Love healing and restoring
No one can touch me in our secret place
For it's an amazing place just for You and me Lord

Longing For Happiness

There is a happiness I long for
I fear I will never have
A happiness I wish to feel
In the morning light
A happiness I want to see
Instead of all this darkness

I long to see my mirrored eyes
I wish not to turn away
I want not to hide behind this mask
For the shame
I consume inside

I desire to know and feel happiness
I wish to accept my emotions and not fear them
I long to trust even one soul to let them in
To feel my shattered heart
For someone to understand my tears and
To show me what love truly is

I so long for happiness each day through
Where I no longer hide behind cold dark walls
Oh, how I fear happiness can't be real

Happiness

Oh how I see and feel the happiness I so longed for
It came from the most understanding and truest Friend
Someone with love and empathy
Someone ever present, and yet concealed

He walked with me each day and
Many times He carried me
Happiness He shares and
Supplies through true friends

Happiness came from Someone
Who knows my every tear
Compassionately sheds them too
Happiness I feel through the love He has always shown

Happiness is in the arms of Jesus,
The Greatest Love Of All
The Greatest Friend ever known

Happiness is knowing that no matter what
Trial, pain, joy or anger lies ahead
That One True understanding Friend
Will always be there walking by my side
And carrying me through to the end

Happiness is sharing my joy and sadness

With One True understanding soul
Happiness I found to be God's amazing Love
And the promise of eternal life by accepting
The sacrifice of his SON

Happiness is found in His Love

Shower

I took a shower trying to wash away all the pain.
Even though I scrubbed and scrubbed as hard as I could,
I couldn't stop feeling dirty or your hands upon me
Trying hard to wash away the nastiness from my body
I still feel from you

I took a shower just trying to wash away the dirtiness
And trash I feel within my soul
But even as the water flows on me, all I feel is dirt
And shivers all over me from what you did to me

How can you be so strong and powerful to make
These horrible feelings remain over me?
To make me feel so much hate for God,you and me?
I take this shower wishing to wash it all away,
But all I feel I can do is stand here with tears flowing
Scrubbing hoping to wash the pain away

I take this shower wishing all my thoughts and
Memories of you would go far away
But no matter how much I scrub or how much I wish
The thoughts of you still remain
Even soap cannot wash away you from me
The dirtiness and shame you placed upon me still stays

No matter how long or how many times I shower,

I cannot wash you and all the awful hurt away
Obviously I am unsuccessful at scrubbing the pain
You placed upon me away, cause all I feel and see
Is all the pain you dug deep in me
All I can do is stand here screaming with tears
Flowing and scrubbing, but nothing goes away
Please I wish at least to scrub the shame away
And never let me see your face again
Oh how I pray the next shower I will succeed to
To wash it all away

The New Shower

I take a shower today with a jump of joy
Yes, it is a new shower
For as I shower I feel the living water
Flowing all over me
A new feeling of life
I feel love filling me as The Father's
Living water is running over me

As I take this new shower today I know
My Savior's river of life is flowing over and in me
As I wash I feel His hands cleansing me
His cleansing blood is pouring over me
Your hands can no longer hold me captive
For you have no power over me anymore
The Savior rescued me

As I shower now it is a new shower
I feel a new life upon me
A deep peaceful feeling overtakes me
As the water runs over me
I know there is no dirt, no nothing that
Remains on me unclean for the Father has
Washed me in the living water
No scrubbing needed for the river of life
Flows on me cleansing me inside and out
Now I take a new shower every day in my
Father's river of life

CHAPTER 3
(ALLOWING RESTORATION OF THE HEART)

Beauty

Beauty living deep within
Locked tightly in chains
Trapped deep from all the brokenness
Slowly crawling along as a caterpillar
Searching for someone to mend my brokenness
Limited by my past and pain
Beauty no longer seen

Crawling along all broken
Tears flowing as my mind, body, and soul reap in the pain
Wishing to be seen instead of stepped on
Darkness all around with shivers of coldness all upon me
Oh how I wish the brokenness gone and beauty seen

Suddenly, crawling slowly along in darkness,
I hear a soft voice asking, "Do you believe?"
As I spoke the word, "Yes," He pulled me close
I feel the warmth of peace and love all around
He lifts my head, wipes my tears, and says,
"I love you my child."
Brokenness removed, beauty unlocked
From this day forward

Mending every part of me

Every speck of dirt washed away
No more scrubbing
No more wondering, “Who am I?”
For as I say “Yes” to the Father,
He pours His Living Water over me
No more brokenness
Flying high and low
Transformed into His beautiful butterfly

Beauty released from deep within
New hopes and dreams alive
No more fiery darts, for I stand on the solid rock
Flying high and low, spreading my wings
Beauty within bursting out, shining, spreading
God's love everywhere
Transformed forever by the Father’s hands
Now, His beautiful butterfly will shine forever
For by the Father's grace, I am saved
Beauty no longer trapped within

Voices

Voices in my head roaring all around
Pounding me with negative thoughts
Feelings of darkness and fierce fire all around me
Voices in my head burning deep within my mind
A force within me keeps those with helping hands
At bay
For the voices in my head, you cannot change
The horror they bring
Now I wonder, will this ever end?

Suddenly, I feel a cool gentle breeze coming
Whirling all around me
Like nothing I ever felt before
The most amazing heavenly aroma filling the air
A calmness and feeling of peace overtakes me
Voices in my head halt as the gentle breeze fills the air
I feel a peaceful presence near
Then suddenly I hear a soft whisper in my ear,
"My child, fight like David!
Stand, throw the stones I have given you.
Believe, beat the giants; they will flee!"
Voices in my head go away forever.

He wraps His arms around me, lifts me up, and says

"You belong, you are loved, now stand, throw the stones
Be that David!
Beat the giants, my child!"
I know now I have the stones to beat
The evil voices in my head
Now the voices become voices of joy, happiness, and
Love

Voices in my head, now you must flee,
For I throw the stones that He has provided
Evil voices in my head, you are defeated
Voices in my head, flee, for I belong, I am loved, and
I am His
I throw the stones, for I am like David
No more voices of evil
No more will your words hurt me, burn me, fill my mind with
Horror,
For I know that His words are the stones that defeat you
Giants, no more of your voices in my head,
For you are defeated
I won this battle; the Father has set me free,
For He gave me
The stones to defeat you long ago
Now, my hands are open to throw the stones He provided
Evil, negative voices in my head, now no more!
I am FREE!

Untouched Spirit

For days on end, you run from your pain
Destroying innocence as you please

Yes, I was a victim, tormented and raped
By your inhuman ways
With eyes closed,
Heart torn in pieces;
My spirit was never taken,
For the Father held it in His Hands

My spirit your violent attacks could not
And will not touch
For the Father saw your fiery darts
Coming fast and furious
He extinguished them with His Mighty Word

Now, with my spirit untouched,
But my body broken, I surrender all
To the Father who mends

So many times, you beat me till
I had no strength but to turn the other cheek
Oh, but the Father lifted me and

Purified me with His cleansing Blood
He took my heart in His Mighty Hand
And stitched it back together again

With my untouched spirit
I continue to sing
His praises
As He mends
You caused me to suffer in your hell,
But my Father held onto my untouched spirit
When I opened my eyes,
I was set free and bound to Him

Yes, We Have A Choice

So many of us never knew who the Trinity was
The ones we thought had power were nothing,
Because they stood for evil
Our will was pushed away, not by the real Father
We know now, no matter what you said or did, we are loved,
Always were by the Trinity
Agony, pain, thirst, abandonment, or distress did not cause us
To ever abandon the Father's will
Jesus's purpose and dream He placed in us will be fulfilled
For yes, we have a choice that matters

Jesus would not allow any temptation
To bring Him down from the cross,
We chose to follow His example
To never allow anyone or anything to stop our purpose
Given by the Father
To serve the Trinity always
His purpose filled, nothing less
It is our choice

Jesus knew death was not the end, but the beginning

Eternity ago,
He chose to let our sins hold Him on the tree
For forgiveness to set us free
So we chose to struggle, go through the abuse,
Feel the evil and blood you
Put on us, because we knew deep within the
"Yes" had a purpose,
And the dream would be fulfilled

Unknown to us, our choice from the beginning
Was being fulfilled never forgotten
His blood was and is our protection
No other blood could cleanse us
Yes, we chose His Blood

The “Begotten Son’s” blood shed
To cleanse all unrighteousness
The choice to follow the Savior has always
Been our choice that matters
His plan to send those needed to present us
Back to the Creator fulfilled
Relationship never broken, only paused for a moment
For darkness to be removed and His light to shine again
As we made a choice
A choice to be free, receive love, give forgiveness, receive
Forgiveness, And most of all free to accept His Salvation
Yes, Free to choose

Broken

I sit here broken
At the end of my rope
Pills in my hand
Looking and praying for an end
My heart is throbbing faster and faster
Thinking of the last beat it will make
My body is so beaten
My heart is torn
There is nothing left to be broken
You can't pull me down any more
For I am at the bottom
And only see one way out
I feel I have nothing left to give, to live for,
Or nowhere to turn
Feeling so forsaken like
I am drowning in pain
Broken and alone

Suddenly, sitting here broken with tears flowing,
I call out for Jesus and a cool
Breeze comes upon my face
I feel a strong presence of
Peace beyond my words
Hands of comfort that I never felt before
Pick me up
Feeling Jesus's presence so real
As never before
Makes me know
Without a doubt, He is the Savior
The pills fall from my hands as our Savior

Wraps me tightly, with His warm embrace
He bottles up each tear for the river of life
Because of His love for me, my life was saved
And your life was too
Jesus is waiting patiently
For each one of us to call on Him
You will then also see and know your life
Was saved the day He died for each one of us
He is the way out of the brokenness

Sparrow

His eyes are on the sparrow

I sing because His eyes are on me

Sing and praise because I am free

Free to feel His love

Free as a sparrow

No longer in this prison

Free to break the chains

Oh how lovely is My little sparrow

The joy of your tiny voice singing to the Father!

Fly free little sparrow, fly free

No longer locked up in pain

Fly and sing little sparrow

For His eyes are on the sparrow

I Couldn't

I couldn't break the chains

I couldn't smash the walls

I couldn't remove my mask

I couldn't be me;

Your rejection overwhelmed me

I couldn't feel love;

Pain engulfed me

I couldn't say no;

On Bluetooth Fear consumed me

I couldn't,

But God could and did for ME!

Blind

I was blind, but now I see

With spiritual eyes beyond the horizon

I can see all God has for me

Faith is not by sight

Faith sees far beyond the rainbow

For if I see with physical eyes only

I am blind and lost

For I cannot see all God has for me

Not through natural eyes, but spiritual eyes

I see truth

Not just facts before me

Facts may not be His Truth

They compel me to Holy Spirit, who is Truth

His Truth erases all my blindness

With spiritual eyes given by Him I see

Blindness no more

You and My Father

You see my tears
And hear my cries
I reach out my hands, but
All you do is turn away
Don't you care for me?
As I plead for your help
You walk away
Why don't you care for me?

As you fade away I feel a cool breeze come upon my face
I hear the words "I love you my child!"
Oh, how I wonder who I hear
Such presence of peace and love
He wipes away my tears
He says He is my Father
Holding me tight
I feel His love and I know He cares for ME

You walk away, but He will never
He is here FOREVER!
That is His promise never to forsake me

I Was I am

I was just a dark little caterpillar
Slowly crawling along all lonely full of darkness
Wondering which way to turn
Do I go up or down, right or left?
Was the right road straight or was it the curved one?
Seems I was always fed something, but never full
Why couldn't my beauty inside be seen?
Why so much misery and darkness all that could be felt?
Just wanted to know the joy of hearing the birds sing
Wanting to soar like an eagle in the sky
Oh, how I wished to taste the salt of the earth
To have one little friend crawl along with me just like
A shadow by my side

Finally I saw, I am not just a caterpillar
Now I know, all along
As I crawled slowly, I had a friend
Feeding me exactly what I needed
My eyes and heart had to be opened to see He was enough
I had to know the provider to know which way to go
My beauty you could not see, for I did not know it till
I saw the Hand that created me
No misery or darkness in His Holy Light
Now I know I will soar like an eagle
Yes, He was always right beside me

Slowly, as my friend and Savior holds me now,
I spin within, flushing away all darkness
My mind is changing, and my heart is flowing with joy
Forgiveness and love overflowing me

I feel the flowing water cleansing me
With a taste of salt is beyond words
For He is the salt of the earth

The hand of my new friend transforming me
Out I push, flying free, all the beauty He
Created me to be, seen through all the darkness
Now I know the light, for I am the beautiful butterfly
He always meant me to be
I see He has always taken care of me!

My Words Have a Voice

My eyes are heavy, but I cannot sleep
For words deep within push to be freed
Words that are a piece of me
Words with expressions of feelings weighed down
By bricks so many of you placed upon me
My words unable to be heard so many times,
Because of fear I allowed as a child to be placed within me,
Only tears seen from my heart of pain
You all inflicted on me
Unspoken words with scars so deep, I could not mend
Words so locked up in chains, for all they are is pain,
Hurt, and love burned away
Your words devoured me

No more! No more! My words are free!
For I am not the victim you sentenced me to be
I am even more than a survivor for I
Am the conqueror God intended
Yes, I know you sentenced me to a
Prison of darkness
Feeling like nothing but sinking sand
All around me on my sinking ship
Sickness striking in every corner
With crippling moments
A void so deep and unknown, I couldn't
Believe or see love was real

Lifting my eyes even through fear of

What would be seen in them
But then, I saw a light shining on the
David in me and heard a whisper,
'It's time to move mountains!"

Now you see i'm standing on Solid Rock not sinking sand
Yes, you broke me in many pieces
Putting many roadblocks in my way over and over,

Trying to stop me, but you never killed my dream,
For the darkness you thought was my sentence
Was a greater light God showered on me
The road blocks were just a moment of rest
Strengthening me to walk the next mile
You believed your evil hands and fiery darts would stop me
They won't!
No more!
My words are now free, for forgiveness has been spoken
For you all
Your eyes of evil, haunting hands and words
Unbearable, no longer hold me in many parts
Of prison in my mind
Chains are broken
Childhood stolen, restored
Now I see the table God set before me
In the presence of my enemies
Greater than what was stolen
My voice is stronger, louder than
A roaring lion

My eyes and ears opened fully to the power
Of our words
One sent to show me the power of the tongue

Yes, He used her to teach,so I would know
Truth to speak
The truth of it all may never be heard, or seen
By all in this earthly realm
But the Father knows
For He mends it all
By His stripes I am healed
Now my words are free and have a voice

Somebody

I am somebody!

You may say I am nobody
God says I am somebody
God says I am His child, so I am somebody
You may say I am different or don't belong
God says I am made in His image
You may have destroyed a part of me
But God gave it back
He loves me no matter what and says
I am somebody

You are nobody, because you chose to inflict pain
You tell me lies, but I chose Truth
From the darkness, now I see the Light
I am somebody, and you can be somebody

When He said, "You are healed and you are SOMEBODY",
I chose to touch the hem of His garment, be healed, and to
Love
I choose to be somebody
Through the eyes of a sparrow, I see, I am somebody!

CHAPTER 4
(THE PROCESS EMBRACED)

Resurrecting The Pierced Heart

My heart pierced intensely day by day with
Squeezing pain
The heart turned quickly to stone
Trapping in all the pain and scars
My heart beating uncontrollably with feelings of fire burning
Continuously, I see your face, I hear your
Words of evil, and feel your hands ripping at me
You raped not only my body but also my mind, and
My soul, sealing the stone all over my heart, not
A crack left
Now my heart with the seal of stone for
Love, peace, joy or anything cannot reach it
For your fingerprint has left nothing but darkness
Stone so heavy my body quivers from the weight

Finally, as the stone continues to weigh me down
My body and mind torn to millions of pieces
I cry out for Jesus to rescue me
I hear
"Take my hand, all I wanted was you to ask"
I reach up as I hear His voice and He asks, me
"My child, will you let me in to remove the stone?"
As I say yes and ask His forgiveness
I feel His grace pour over me
I feel the chisel in His hands
Cracking the stone away
Yes! A new river of life flowing to me

The pain and hurt you caused me

Falling in His hands
As I speak each of your names giving you forgiveness,
The Father and my Savior
Swiftly chisel the stone away
Every piece removed as He takes my heart in His hand
Molding and wiping all darkness away
A fresh flow of blood rushing through me as
He resurrects my old pierced heart with
His fresh new breath of life
My heart filled with love unknown before
Resurrected with the new promised eternal life

Transformation

A journey beyond your dreams
A journey deep within yourself
Bringing out the complete real you
Freeing the person God made

It is a journey of letting go of old baggage
Transformation changing you inside and out
It is not a temporary change;
Not a change in what you wear
But a much deeper and greater change
It is a complete transformation

Transformation is a coming home
A willingness to be set free;
Throwing out all that is old and dead
Transformation is a true
Breathing to wholeness and healing
Shifting out of inner criticism,
Letting God cleanse you, so now
You can acknowledge your true self

Now an awakening out of darkness
To the light of your true nature
Transformation gives you true new sight
A sight beyond what you can see
With your natural eyes

It is seen only with your inner eyes;

The spiritual eyes God gave you
Transformation transcends fear and
Turns suffering into liberation

Transformation is a process which takes time
A process that is not all full of joy
Transformation is breaking down and letting go
Transformation is a complete washing by
The Father's Hands inside and out
Holding my head high, knowing I am being
Transformed by the greatest Hands of all
Into whom God says I am...
The Father's new beautiful butterfly

Into His Hands

The Begotten Son knocks at the door of our heart asking us
To trust just as He did Committing
His soul into His Father's hand
Now He asks us, are we willing to commit ourselves
Fully into His hands, not into the dark unknown,
Nor into the grave or a void, but into the
Hands of our Father knowing
Life He gives is forever nothing lost
Jesus doesn't want an inch He wants it all, for
He gives nothing less,
But the choice is ours
A mustard seed of faith is all it takes
Then watch the young eagle become the soaring eagle
He was created to be
Into His hands commit your spirit as you surrender,
All receiving
His love

Stop taking back the wheel, commit all to Him
You keep asking Jesus take this habit, anger, rage, doubt,
problem, and bitterness, but you don't fully give it
Stop trying to hide from the issues and let
God bring you through
He doesn't take it unless you give and release all
Into His Father's hands He committed Himself,
Now it's your turn
Stop blaming God for your mistakes
Bad things happen, you blame God, but it was not His fault
You closed Him off
You took matters back in your own hands

Now it's time to let go and put it all into His hands
Trust,commit it all into His hands, for the life and love He has For us is real

You wake in the morning light, but do not acknowledge Jesus
Even with a whisper
You go all day till time to lay down and rest your eyes Without even
One word to Him or even His name unless you feel fear
A problem; then you say "If you're there Lord I need your Help!"
Why, when His Word with all the answers sits on a table Covered
With dust, picked up and read when you feel a need
Speak to Him always, He is waiting

You pray when you feel a need and He still answers, but
You do not listen or you do not accept the answers
You listen to praise and worship and sing a little song, but You
Never let it move you just words from your mouth
God does not want you to make someone think you know Him
It's not a show, it's a commitment
He doesn't want religion
Into His hands surrender all

Suffering is part of life and growth that draws
You nearer to the Father
He wants to be near always rather good times or bad

Stop turning off and on the light instead put your thoughts
Back on Him
Into His hands commit your soul; just as the Son did on the
Cross of
Love and grace
Into His Hands!

Breath of Life

The lord breathed a new life into you
Breathe in His mercy and His grace daily
Receive the breath of life
He has given you a new life
Life more abundant
Rejoice for the Lord reigns in your heart forever
You are His special child
Rejoice as He rejoices with you
As He breathed that breath back in you

Now He is removing those stones that weighed you down
You are free!
Live now under the Father's banner of freedom
For He holds you with His compassion

Rejoice again He says rejoice
He has breathed his life into you
Inhale him, take Him in,
Breathe out the pain, anger and resentment
For you are free
Free to be you
You are somebody

The pain is fading
For the Lord has begun a new thing
Release the pain completely now it is His not yours
For you are His special child
He gave you a new life when you accepted Him
He breathed His mercy and grace into you
The evil they did will hurt no more

For the lord says "It is meant for good"
Smile now from the depths of your heart
For the pain and sorrow is washed away
Rejoice now with praises
For He has breathed a new life everlasting into you

Living Word

Living Word moving me inside and out
Stirring deep within my soul
The True Word that will never die
Living Word that communicates to all
It penetrates to the soul and spirit
Changing attitudes of the heart
Divine Word opening eyes from spiritual
Blindness into words full of light
It is alive, Living Word

As I praise, speak, dance or read,
The Living Word comes more alive in me
For life is in His Testimonies
The Living Word that moves and proclaims the Truth
The Truth comes from the Savior of us all
Words that will change you
His Words are alive

The Living Word full of stories that bring
Life, peace, truth, and healing
Full of joy, happiness, sadness, hope, light and darkness
Words that show even pain always leads to fulfillment
Of peace by the Father
Living Word that shows death leads to
New beginnings, eternal life has no end
The Word full of every emotion
A guide given by the Father
The only tool you will ever need
The Living Word
The Living Word leads us to our divine purpose

His true Word will carry you through it all
The Word is alive never to die
Always proclaiming The Father, Son and Holy Spirit
Living Words always leading us to praises
It is full of every answer
It tells the beginning and the end
It is the Bible, the Living Word

The Door

Oh! How I wish for you to open the door to the true Light
It's all your choice
Open the door and you will find the secret place
With My Father
He waits patiently for you to take the hand of The Only
Begotten Son
Listen closely
You will hear the soft little knock at the door of your heart
The choice is yours
If you open the door let Him in, Eternal Life is yours forever
The Father's light will remove the surrounding darkness
Please my friend accept the Light of the world
Open the door and feel His embrace
Feel the most amazing love
The choice is darkness or light
Open the door to the Light and close the door to darkness
Eternal life or the fire of hell forever
Now my friend
The choice is yours
Which Door?

You Don't Know Me

You know of Me, but you don't know Me
You feel Me in the wind,
But you don't recognize it is Me
You serve, but you don't serve Me
You say you love, but you don't love with
Complete real love, for you only know of Me

Yes, you pray, and I hear your prayers
I answer, but you don't hear for you don't know My voice,
You don't know Me
Many times the answer I place right in front of you,
But you can't see it,
Because you're looking for the wrong answer
If you would just have a little talk with Me
And listen you would know My answer
And why

You don't know Me, only of Me
Your ears are deaf to Me
Your eyes are blind
If you would just believe and begin to know Me
Your eyes and ears would be open to Me
Look at me through My creation, the flowers and the trees
See Me, hear Me, I Am Alive, I Am Real
I am here and everywhere

You say you want change and that's good,

But My answer is transformation
For to truly know Me is to be transformed,
Not just changed
My hands will mold every inch of you
Cleansing your heart washing you

In My River of Life
Giving you My body and My blood
Transforming you to who I made you to be
But you choose to only know of Me

You say you believe in Me, but you only
Believe in the story of My death and resurrection
You don't see I am alive here with you now
You don't receive My healing, because you don't
Know I am still healing, I am still here
You only believe in a story, and you only
Believe I am in heaven
You don't see Me at your table, or at your door
Because you only know of Me
I am alive, I walk with you daily asking you
To look up and see Me, know Me, I am the
Answer to it all.
Know Me, not of Me no more
I live, I am here, know Me, see Me, hear Me

My Story

A chapter begins and a chapter ends
My story continues on
Unfolding the past and the present
Unlocking memories deep within that bind
My story has a future
The Father unfolds the pages

The Father knew my story before
He placed me in my mother's womb
A woman who would hold me for only a little while,
But carry the name "mother" forever

He knew the journeys I would endure
He knew every tear, laugh, cry, smile and heartache
He knew the path was full of sorrow and grief
He knew each loss I would face;
The Father knew my story
Before it began

He knew my dreams and desires
He placed them within me
The Father knew who He would use
To show me a dad's heart and
A mom's love for their child

Through it all, He knew my story
Would bring me to take His hand
He knew I would run the race and
Never give up though my soul stumbled
The Father knew I would trust Him and

Meet Him at the foot of the cross
Through my story
I would know He carries me

He would wipe away every tear and
Fill my heart with joy unknown
Through my story,
I would know His love is worth it all

Victory, I will attain in my story;
I am not a victim
My destiny from the Father is part of my story
My story continues on …

Though at times I am hurt, frustrated, and
Tired of the fight,
I know my Father is taking Me to new heights
Restoration is part of my story

I will no longer ask why the pain or sorrow,
I know it's part of my story and
The Father has a plan that carries me through

Love, joy and happiness are also part of my story
My story doesn't end here
It carries on
It's not my story,
It's His

Dad and My Heavenly Father

Dad see my tears
And hear my cries
I reach out my hands, but
All you do is turn away
Don't you care for me?
As I plead for your help
You walk away
Why don't you care for me?
Aren't you my Dad?

As you fade away, I feel a cool breeze come upon my face
I hear the words, " I love you My child."
Oh how I wonder who I hear
Such a presence of peace and love
He wipes my tears away
He says He is My True Father
Holding me tightly
I feel His love, and I know He cares for ME
You walked away, but He will never leave me
He is here FOREVER!
That is HIs promise never to forsake me
He is my Heavenly Father

CHAPTER 5
(NEW LIFE)

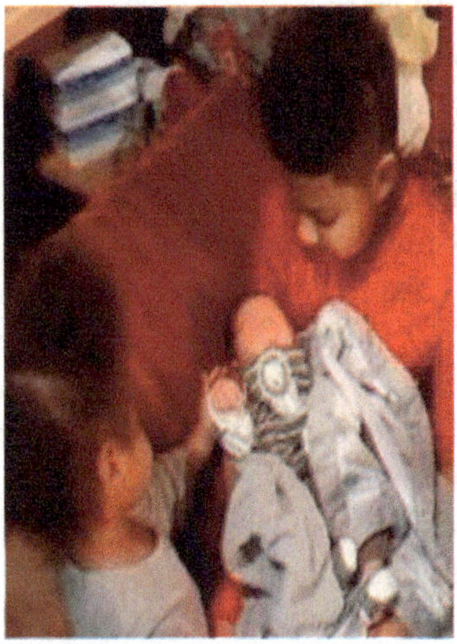

Scars

Scars you see tell a story
They remind me of many things
I know when you see a scar on me you think of hurt
But don't, for most of all
They remind me of the greatest love of all
Scars remind me we are the Father's
Masterpieces molded by the Potter's hands

Scars remind me of the pain inflicted on me by others
Some scars especially on my heart and mind
Remind me of much evil
The price for my scars though was nothing
Compared to the gift I received
Because of the Savior's scars, I am His
Masterpiece molded by His hands
From a broken vessel to FREEDOM

My scars are no longer painful, for now
The few that remain remind me even more of
Forgiveness and love
The scars tell a story of past hurts that
Have been changed to scars of love, for
My Father taught me forgiveness and true love
I know by the Master's hands the protrusions, scars,
And blemishes that remain will finally be fully removed
To reveal His masterpiece in me

You see my scars tell a story of pain and love

But the greatest and deepest scars of all are the ones
That remain forever on our Savior, for they are
The scars of the greatest mission
Scars on His hands and feet we placed upon our
Savior that He willingly took, so we each could
Know the Trinity and make them known
The Trinity… the greatest mission of all

So now, when I look at my scars I see love
No ugliness or pain remain
My scars, healed by love from the Potter's hands
And forgiveness from my heart
Yes, my scars tell a story, and the best part is
It's a story of Love that's part of the greatest mission

He Will Take It All

Pain felt by all
Screeching, horrible pain,
Feeling unbearable at times
But our pain is only a little of what
The Savior endured
Our pain will never compare to His nail pierced hands
The heavy Cross that willingly He carried,
With stripes on His body from beatings and thorns
On His head
He willingly took it all

Now I know the Father's love,
For He washed the pain away with His cleansing Blood
So much more gained than pain could ever take away
Contentment that only comes from our savior
The slight cost of our pain is nothing
Compared to what we gain
I would walk each step of trial and pain again
To reach the Love gained
For I know He will take it all,
Just as He did at the Cross

In faith not asking why

I know the end result
The Father will carry through
The rope will not break, even on its last thread,
For it is the Father's thread pulling me in
No hand will slip,
For His hands cover all pulling closer to Him,
Giving the courage and desire to push on
When the pain seems unbearable,
Look to your Savior and remember;
He will take it all

All spots of dirt removed as we give forgiveness
To those who caused any hurt,
And forgiveness given to us by the Father for holding on,
Replacing pain with love,
Filling me with peace unending,
As I stand in the new River of Life.
For no longer is the Son's pain in vain,
For it is not ours but His.
For He takes it all.
Now the focus is for my reward; the Savior of us all.

Handprints

Handprints are always being left around the world
Everywhere someone goes
Yes, they wash away or fade, but not the
Greatest handprints of all
For everywhere you look you will see the
Father's handprints for He made it all,
Even each unique handprint that passes by your way
So, each place you look and see a handprint, just remember
It belongs to your Heavenly Father, and so even
Though we each go away, our handprints really remain, for
They are part of the Father's, who remain forever

Just as our handprints have been imprinted on your life,
Yours have been etched everywhere you have gone,
For you leave a handprint or two from God
Every time you give a hug, it makes us smile,
For we know you just left a handprint on our shoulder
So, we could feel and see another glimpse of God
Your handprints are special and unique in some way
Or form, just as each of those around you
For your handprints are here to stay, for they are the
Father's handprints

Each handprint special and unique, for the

Father created them to be
Handprints a reminder of the greatest handprints of all,
From the one who molded them one and all
So, now when you see a handprint or two, just remember
It is God's handprints for us all to say,
"I love you my daughter, my son, my sister, my brother,"
"My bride"

So now we leave you a reminder of our handprints with love,
But most of all to remind you God's
Handprints are the largest
And the greatest of all, for they are our
Handprints joined as one

The Father's Words

My heart I give to my child to be My bride
Let My heart flow through the Living Water in you
Let My joy and happiness overflow you inside and out
For the wind of My breath overtakes you
Dig no more for I Am right here carrying you through
The road ahead is straight
I am with you
Though the road behind was curved, I was with you
Now feel My heart beat for you with love
Feel My breath overtake and fill each of My children
New life, new beginnings, and new journeys
Know My love, for it is true love, amazing love, washing
Away all else
My hands change all
For evil is only the size of a grain of sand
Now My children go over the mountain
The new journey lies ahead
My heart beats for you

Embrace

Oh Holy Spirit let me feel Your Embrace
Loving Father wrap Your Arms tightly around me
Never let me go
How I love to feel Your warm Embrace
My sins forgiven through Your Grace,
Embrace me with Your Love
My past washed clean
Oh Father, how I love to feel and know Your Grace

Encircle me with Your warm, loving embrace
Help me grab every thought of You my Provider
Even in a storm, let me embrace You my Lord,
For I know You will lead me through
Oh Father, you are everything I need and want
Let me hold captive every word that is from You

As I look at the sun, the moon, and the stars,
I embrace all of You
Even as I look at the lovely trees,
Smell the sweet flowers,
And see their beauty,
I clutch hold of all of You
As I feel the wind pass around me,
The rain on my head,
Or the sun on my face,
Oh how I feel so much more of You and
Surely know You embrace me

May Heaven's gates open wide

As we embrace
Wrap me in Your Arms
Hold me tightly as I embrace Your Healing Power
Let me feel You to the depths
Of my soul
Oh Father, hold me tightly
May I never let go
Of Your tight
Embrace

Rain On Me

As your rain falls on me washing me clean,
Every spot of dirt falling from me
Your river of raindrops flowing all over me
As I am singing praises, let Your river of life
Flow on me
River of life rain on me

Rain on me Lord Jesus
Pour down on me
Let Your river flow washing me clean
Yes! Pour all of your rain on me
Let the river of tears turn to joy
Rain on me

As I feel Your river flowing, my heart beats faster
My blood flows freely
Being lifted high in your arms
Lord, let your new rain continually fall on me
River of life pouring from my Father's hands,
Rain on me

Rain on me Lord Jesus
Pour down on me
Let your river flow washing me clean
Yes, Pour all of your rain on me
Let the river of tears turn to joy
Rain on me

Your raindrops falling everywhere

Let me stand my hands opening wide
Let me feel Your presence
Your arms wrapping around me
Smelling the freshness of Your breath
Flowing through each droplet of rain
Flowing from that river of tears
Now full of peace
Father rain on me!

Rain on me Lord Jesus
Pour on me
Let Your river flow washing me clean
Yes! Pour all of your rain on me
Let the river of tears turn to joy
Rain on me

Life

In the soup bowl of life,
We find joy, pain, happiness, sadness and love
Our earthly lives are filled with daily toil
Life seems empty at times -
Times of depression and loneliness
Life can be a mystery

Life changes, but is never lost
When we accept Jesus' gift
For He is the Light and Bread of Life
He is Glory and the Breath of life
Life is a gift

Life contains joys that
Helps make this a lovely day
But nothing lasts forever
Save the love of Jesus

Life contains pains that
Cause despair and regret
But nothing lasts forever
Save the love of Jesus

Life has a price that
Seems not worth the cost
But Jesus paid the highest price…
His Life!

Jesus is the light and purpose in life

When we forfeit houses, family, or property, for His sake,
We will receive a hundred times as much
And will inherit eternal life

Life is Jesus

Breathe On Me

Breathe on me, Lord Jesus every moment
Yes, breathe on me
When I wake, let me feel You breathe on me
As I walk in the morning sun,
As I run in the night,
Let me feel Your breath on me
As I sleep, breathe on me

Lord let me smell the aroma of Your breath
All around me as You breathe on me
Let me feel Your breath blow all over me
Your breath so refreshing, cool, warm, gentle,
A breath that so overtakes me as You
Breathe on me
Let me smell Your aroma that is sweeter than the
Lilies in the valley
Breathe on me

As I see You in the sky, through the moon and the stars,
Let me feel You breathe on me
Lord, as I cry out in pain and feel You,
Wipe away my tears breathe on me
Without Your breath, healing ceases
So Lord breathe on me Your
Breath of peace and healing power

Breathe on me, Lord,

For as You breathe on me, I feel a freshness of
Living water flow through me
A cleansing heart You breathe in me
Breathe on me Your eternal life, for death
Cannot take the breath You breathe on me
Your breath gives life unending
Breathe on me, for Your breath overtakes me
With Your love unending, filling me with all of You
Breathe on me as I pass fully in Your arms

The Ocean

The ocean is a treasure box full of our Father's creation

As I sit and survey the beauty of the ocean,
I see the Creator
Listening to the water rushing in, I hear Him
Tasting the salty air, I feel
His Healing Power, His Peace, His Joy

As I hear the ocean rushing in,
The Father is calling me into His Presence
I feel the water flowing all around and over me
Washing me clean with waves of
His Love, His Cleansing, His Tranquility

Oh how I see God's Glory reflected on the ocean
As the waves rise, I see His Power
Lifting and carrying me over storms, rushing in
His Healing Power, His Love, His Calmness

As I sit and listen to the calming waves,
I feel the Father pouring His Peace upon me
I feel the Creator wrapping His Healing Arms around me

Suddenly, I hear the Father whisper,
"Who takes care of the ocean?"
As I realize the answer and salty tears flow,
He declares, "You are My Creation too!"

Were You There?

These three words asked so many times
The words the Lord Jesus hears and answers over,
And over, and over
Words He clearly understands,
But three words He will never ask you
For He knows you were there
He took your hand, held you close,
And carried your sins with Him to the Cross

He was there to feel your confusion,
As He asked the Father, "Why have you forsaken me?"
The Father knows the Son was there
To fulfill the ancient plan
His Father took His hand, held Him close,
And forgave your sins on the Cross
Yes, He was there

He was there to feel your anguish
As soldiers whipped and tore His skin
He took your hand, held you close,
When their leather paddle, scarred without and within
Yes, He was there

He was there to feel your suffering,
As He stumbled with the Cross
He took your hand, held you close,
When He was knocked to the ground
Kicked, and stomped, and bruised
Yes, He was there
He was there

To shield that life ending blow
To interrupt that fatal bullet
To remove the shame of rapes
There to take the pain and let you know that this
Was not His plan
Yes, He was there

He was there
To speak loving truth to words that cut so deep
"No one wants you; you're fat, ugly, and stupid!"
"You are worthless!"
There to tell you those are not His words
For you are made in His image and your identity is in Him
Yes, He was there

He was there
When you rejected Him
When you walked by someone in need
Asking your many questions
He answered your non listening ears
When you said "No,"
He was still there knocking
Waiting patiently for your reaching hand
Yes, He was there

He was there
To carry your baby home to the Father
To show you a way out of the fire

To hear every cry
To hold every tear
Yes, He was there

He sees, knows and understands,
For He felt
Despair, abuse, and rejection
He was there to rescue you
By going to the Cross
Yes, He was there

He was there
Feeling His Father's love
Breathe life back into Him,
Raising Him from the grave
He then breathed life into you,
Revealing Trinity's love
For Their Divine purpose was, is, and will be fulfilled
Yes, He was there

He was there
To wipe away your every tear
To grasp your reaching hand
To have and to hold forevermore
Now, no longer their wills win, but His will
For you took the Lord's hand, and
Yes, He was there

He was, is, and always will be there
For better or for worse
Using all to fulfill His Divine purpose.

So the answer to those three often asked words is,

Yes! You were there!

Tabernacle

A place where you make my words known and always living
In the Tabernacle they will know the living God
A place to come to and feed the hunger of
Their hearts and souls
A place for you to feed my people
A place my covenant of love is made
The place you will show them my mercy,
Strength, and healing power

You lead them to a place in the
Tabernacle where they will know I Am
My Holy Spirit always in this place,
Because I Am always in you
The Father is always in this Tabernacle to guide us
To the light of his calling
From within the nest of this Tabernacle many shall grow

A place to worship free before the throne of God
Dancing and singing their praises to the King of Kings
The truth is seen within this Tabernacle of Faith
A place I will always dwell
A place where you keep religion out and the Truth in
In this Tabernacle of Faith you share a glimpse of Heaven

CHAPTER 6
(THE UNBORN)

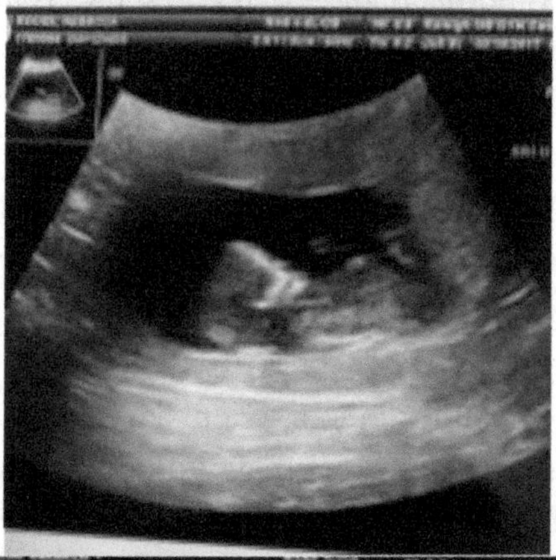

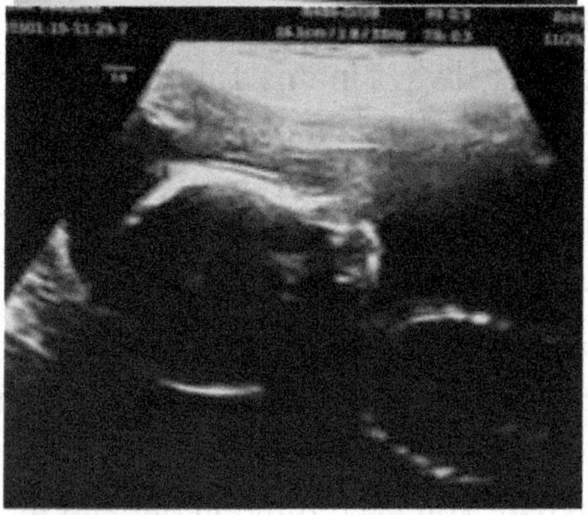

I Am Alive

I am alive, please feel me, hear me
Just for a moment I wish you could hear my voice
I wish you could hear my cry
Yes, I am alive within you
I have a heart and a soul
I am special just as you are special
For our Father created us all

Slowly I am growing within you
Why do you wish to kill me?
I hear your sadness and anger
That I am here
Please don't destroy me
The Father has a purpose for me
Please answer my cries
I am alive!

I could be a doctor, nurse, or teacher,
Or maybe even a preacher
Don't you want to hear me call you mama?
I can't wait to feel you hold me in your arms
Oh how I wish to see your loving eyes,
And see the smile upon your face
I am alive!

Wait, no please don't end my life!

Yes, it's your choice
Please, I am alive!
I am a gift from our Father
Please don't end this chance
The Father gave me to serve Him fully

I guess you made your choice
Back into The Father's hands I go
Never to see the world you know
Never to know your love,
But I will always know My True Father
Into His hands now I remain
I am Alive!

Author, Unborn Child

I Dream

As I lay here in this warm comfortable
Ball of water, I dream
Yes, for hours upon hours I dream
My dreams are so full of great
Imagination
Oh, what will it be like when they
Finally hold me in their arms?
I may only be a tiny baby inside you, but
I am alive and I dream
I dream of the day we meet face to face
I dream of all the things I hear about
Maybe I will be a doctor like you, or a police
Officer like your friend
Yes, I dream as I listen to your voice
Wondering what you look like
Oh, I know you are beautiful
For now I belong to you
I dream of things we will do together
Yes, I can't wait for you to see all
My little fingers and toes
Feel me moving and know that I
Am here dreaming of you
Oh, please just let me dream
Wait my heart is slowing
I feel strange
Why have you chosen to take my life,
To kill my dream?
I am happy you got a chance to be somebody
So happy someone chose to let your
Dreams remain alive

There is one dream you could never kill
It is still alive and real
My dream is real for I am back in my
Father's hands
"I forgive you"
I dream!

Little One I Never Knew

My precious little one,
I never knew you were within me
Til the moment I saw your lifeless body,
So still, not a sound, with blood all around

Never allowed
To see you move
To hold you
To feel your little heartbeat
To show you love that I never knew from a mother

Never a chance
To show you that I would hold you safe
And hide you from the evil hands I felt...
Little one I never knew
Please know, I love you

My unborn child
I am so sorry the evil will of others deprived you and me of
Your life,
Yet grateful they never could have you,
And that you are free

My precious little one,
I wish I could have seen
Your beautiful bright eyes, even for a moment
Longing even more to touch you,
To rock you in my arms,
To hold you close,
And let you hear the words

"I love you!"

My unborn child,
Your life ended within me, yet didn't end
Even though I mourned for you,
I rejoice the Father saved you
Your life with me is delayed,
Until we're rejoined in Heaven with the Savior

Little one I never knew,
Oh how, I wish I could have celebrated your first breath,
Even for a moment, but your true Father did,
As He wrapped you in His, arms and
You took your first breath back with HIm

I know now little one, the Savior protected you
You were His first just as I am His too
Thankful you never had to feel sorrow, anger,
Sadness, hatred, or even fear
Never to feel the hands of evil ones
For the Savior knew before you came into this world
He would rescue you
Only love for you to feel in your life my precious child
I love so dear
Even though I never got to know you

I wish I had at least a copy of a fingerprint to remember you
For now all I have is one image and memory to know you
An image and memory that saddens my heart
I would have done anything to protect you my little one,
If I just knew you were there
So, thankful the Savior knew

I hold on now and look forward to the moment our Savior
Will place you in my hands to hold you tight
And I will feel that little heartbeat
Well, for now I will carry you in my heart
Looking forward to the day those words will no longer be
“I never knew you my precious little one”
I will know the gift you were meant to be
It won't be long, but I have to finish the job the Father
Has for me,

We Win precious one
Now, my child I release you up to Jesus,
And I know He has placed you in His Father’s Hands
I love you my little one I never knew, but cherish the day I
Will

Plan B

Plan B: Just another way to stop life from beginning
Yes, it is another clear free will choice made so available to
All
A plan created by scientists who think nothing of life
Plan B gives you permission to not even think of the choices
You are making just the pleasure that you can have for now
A simple little pill created to prevent you hopefully
From becoming
Pregnant

Yes, it is your body, but it was created by God
In His image, and
To be His temple
Never did He give us the right to take away life
Yes, you had the right to choose, to do the things
That caused you
To conceive, but not the right to prevent or
Kill after the matter
Plan B: Just another way of abortion, sad to say

Yes, you rush off making sure you prevent a problem you
See rushing through your mind
So worried... what if …
Then you begin to think about your parents and know
The solution has to be Plan B
Never once did you think of your choice being wrong till
after The fact
Now all you say as tears roll down your checks,
And you swallow
This little pill is

"Thank you Jesus"
But, please don't, for He was not a part of this
Jesus never provided a wrong way out

Plan B: The world's way of covering up free-will choices
Just remember, your choices are your own not the Father's,
And
If a life was stopped quickly by Plan B, our Heavenly Father
Knew
And swept that little one right back up in His hands right by
His heart
Plan B never prevents the Father from His work, for He has
Proven
That little pill has failed many times, for a
Scientist cannot destroy God's work with Plan B

CHAPTER 7
(DEDICATED TO INFLUENCERS)

Looking Through Your Eyes

Looking through your eyes, I see the world so differently
You do not get caught up in lies
You see everything through the Father's eyes
You see the beauty within

You see beauty through the ugliness
You see the hurt pouring through their eyes
You are there to comfort their cries
Through Your eyes, I see a pain untold

You love others as they are
You see things I never see
You know of healing from the brokenness
Through Your eyes, I see a love unknown

You opened my eyes to a world mysterious
You see the reality within
You see I can trust again
Through Your eyes, I see the Father's amazing love

Looking through Your eyes I see the true love
Of Christ and the meaning of the best love ever...
Salvation

Victory Is Ours

We continue to press through the journey put before us
For we know the Victory is ours!
Every chain placed upon us removed
All marks and scars made by the enemy gone
Washed away by the Father's hand
Memories that remain are like a picture on a wall
Only to remind us of our Father's true love
Showing us of where we've been
And each trial He brought us through
Victory is ours

Now to continue our destiny and purpose
Victory is yours and mine
This part of our life's journey the Father chose
For us to run and finish together
Though the enemies attack us they will not win
We will continue the race never giving up
We know the end result
We will cross this finish line together
That is His promise
Victory is mine and victory is yours
Just hold on to the Father's hand
He will lead us through

Remember this race is worth every step of the way

The Father's glory to be revealed through us, and in us
Victory we sing
Victory we dance
For victory is ours
Victory, We win!

The Father is always reminding us He hasn't forgotten or left us
Giving us signs or words to remind us of His promises
He said,
"Call to Me, and I will answer you, and show you
Great and mighty things, which you do not know."
(Jeremiah 33:3 ESV)
Keeping us together to finish a race and begin anew
The Father has bound us together for many reasons
This Victory is ours given by the Father

Never to despair for when one of us needs a little extra hand,
The Father sends a little more guidance our way
Using each of us for one another's healing
Sometimes to give a little courage,
Or to hold a hand,
To give that much needed extra push,
And especially to share a little more needed love,
But most of all to give guidance back
To the Father
We cross this finish line hand in hand with our Father

Victory! Victory we win!
The end of this journey is here

Time to see more of His glory
"For we know that the sufferings of this
Present time are not worthy to be compared
With the glory which shall be revealed in us." (Romans 8:18 ESV)
Restoration and resolution done
Time to cross this finish line and
Walk in the newness of our life,
With victory in Jesus
The Father already won it,
For you and me.
Victory!

Wounded Hearts

Soaring into the world through each day with
Wings of an eagle
Covering those with broken hearts with love Unknown
Helping those with broken wings to heal
Always helping one more to see the truth Unknown
Helping many to hear the voice of the Father
As He watches His little sparrow
Soaring through the world like an eagle
Helping hearts to heal
Helping a rose to bloom

You see the beauty within
Loving them for who they are, not who they think they are
Helping wounded hearts to heal
Helping them to see the beauty that came from The ashes
And that healing is for every part - mind, body, and soul
You unearth all pain
To show us the lies within
Helping broken hearts to heal

You find so much joy in pleasing the Father
Sharing God's loving hand with others
Caring with edifying and encouraging words
For all those who come in your presence
Feel and see the unconditional love of the Father
Helping others see the Light

Storms may come as you soar,

Helping wounded hearts to heal
But drawing on your faith, you soar
With conquering spirit, like an eagle,
Helping wounded hearts to heal
Through the storms, leading many to Christ
To know the love unknown
For wounded hearts do HEAL

Father's Gift

The Father's gift to me,
A much needed spiritual "Mother"
So much more than just a loving, caring friend
Someone to show me a true
Mother's love unknown before
Most of all to draw me to His amazing love

A woman after God's own heart
Spreading the Father's love wherever you go
Drawing many closer to the Father's hands
Pushing for healing and for many to know
The most amazing love of all

You carry the presence of His peace and love,
Even as the storms whirl all around
His praises within you
You feel the pain and discouragement at times,
But continue to give encouragement for you know the reward
Holding on tightly to the Father's promises
Helping others to also become beautiful butterflies
And know the most amazing love of all

Wherever you walk the Father's presence is felt
Seen by the twinkle He placed in your eyes
Reflection of His love clearly shown through you
You see us all through the Father's eyes
Giving of yourself unselfishly so others can know
The most amazing love of all

For now a love unknown before is seen

Felt far beyond the rainbow
Through you many have and will see
The greatest love of all
Many more to stand victorious because you served
You are an amazing gift

Now we win together my mother, my friend
A new journey to begin
Through His amazing love now we soar
With wings of an eagle
Thankful for such an amazing servant for
Our Father

Set Free

Free as a bird
Death has set you free
Fly free now
The past will hurt you no more
Mother dear be free
The past will hurt you no more
For death has set you free
Fly free now for you are set free

Treasures in You

Your smile so uplifting
A smile that will never be lost
When people look at you they feel a leap of joy
They see your smile and know happiness
Is all over you inside and out
Your smile shows the Lord lives in you
For it shows the Father's peace
Your smile brings joy and laughter
For it's only one of the treasure within you

Your hands so willing to help someone in need
Hands used to give a much needed hug
Your hands the Father uses to mold those little ones
The hands to give a clap of cheer when no one else does
Yes, my friend, your hands another treasure a part of you
Your hands a treasure that touches hearts,
And are used by the Father for healings
The Father smiles back at you because
Your treasures aren't stored within but used for joy

Your heart so full of love from the Father,
That every time someone looks into your eyes
They feel His heart of love
The Father uses the mended treasure of your heart,
To help mend the hearts of others
Your heart of treasure never afraid to love

You are a treasure from the Father to hold onto forever

A treasure that even in your struggles,
Your faith is felt strong;
For you know He mends all
Because you use the treasures given to you,
The little ones will sing,
And know the biggest treasure of all in you
Is the Trinity who treasures us all

The Garden

A woman who is after God’s own heart
A woman reflecting the beauty of Our Father above
In the many gardens she plants
A woman who plants seeds in the special garden of our souls
And waters and nurtures like her own

Just as you plant a garden,
God plants a garden in you of love that
You share so abundantly
Just as you nurture your garden,
God nurtures you
Just as the garden reaps what you sow,
So does your life and the lives into which you sow,
Just like removing the weeds from your garden,
You help to remove the weeds in the lives of others

So much beauty seen in you
From the seeds that God sowed in you
Joy you get in sharing and showing God's truth
The reflection of The Lord shone through
The beauty of your life
Is even greater than the garden you grow

You show healing is for everyone…
Body, mind, and soul
And God desires for us to be whole
Through your garden of friendship we all grow
Spiritually, emotionally, and physically

Thank you for sharing your many gardens, especially your
Garden of God’s love

Prepare

I never could prepare for this day
Only the Heavenly Father knew
You were going on your final journey
To your forever home… Destiny
Death you never got to see
For I know Jesus took your hand
Led you home to the place
He prepared for you
When it's time with my place prepared,
I will meet you there

Though you left for the promised land too early
You are still within my heart
Thankful for the gift that you were part of our family
Wish I could have prepared
Knowing it would be the last time
I would travel the long road to see you

I want to hear you laugh again
To see a smile upon your face
I know I will again one day
For I believe in the Savior
Who took you to Paradise

Though my pain is great I know
You are alive and free
All your sorrow wiped away
Even though I didn't get to prepare for this time
My heart now prepares to one day see you…Alive
Now I hold to our memories even more

Cherishing them all
They were part of our journey together
The Father had prepared for us
Now your journey here has fully ended
Mine carries on with you close at heart
My tears will fade and pain will ease
As I hold on knowing you are
With the Father… Alive
Now my heart prepares to see you again

A Rose Reborn

As the pages of life unfold
Every moment past, present, and future
He holds

With every speck of time a treasure to unfold
Even through the thorns
A new rose has been born

For you were never lost from His sight
Just a bud waiting to bloom
For He creates beauty from ashes

Just as a potter molds his clay
The Father molded you
Not one mistake He ever makes

A journey planned just for you
Without trials and sorrows, but sin intruded
And like Job you endured

You know not what tomorrow brings
But you know who holds tomorrow
You know who holds you

Now the rose continues to bloom
As you rest in His arms of peace
His love abounds

For the oil of His Presence

Has now become your essence
You are His rose reborn

Amazing Love

The Father's gift to me
A much needed understanding friend
Even more than that
A loving caring spiritual "Mother"
Helping to feel the love unknown from a mother
Most of all to draw me to the Savior's amazing love

A woman after God's own heart
Spreading the Father's love wherever she goes
Drawing many closer to the potters' hands
Pushing for healing and for all to know the most amazing
Love of all

You carry the presence of His peace and His love
Even as the storms whirl all around
His praises you sing
You feel the pain and discouragement, but
Continue to give encouragement for you know the light
Holding on tight to the Father's promises
So that others can also become His beautiful butterfly
And know the most amazing love of all

Wherever you go the Father's presence is felt
Seen by the twinkle He placed in your eyes
Reflection of His love shown through you
For you see through the Father's eyes
Giving of yourself unselfishly so others can know
The Father's amazing love

A love unknown before is seen and
Felt far beyond the rainbow
For through you, many have and will
Know the greatest gift of all
Eternal life His amazing love
Many to stand victorious because of His gift of a friend
To show and give His amazing love
We win soaring with wings of an eagle
Because of His amazing love

Helping Broken Wings to Heal

Soaring into the world with wings of an eagle,
Spreading God's Word

High above the clouds you soar like a mother bird

Searching, praying and teaching others to appreciate life

As a newborn chic

Feeding the hungry with God's Word and praying for the
Sick

Helping broken wings to heal

Storms come as you soar above the clouds

Drawing on faith you rise above it all,
Searching through the crowds

Looking for more lost people to carry to your
Nest underneath the Cross

Your conquering spirit like an eagle giving inspiration and

Encouragement to the lost

Helping broken wings to heal

With wings spread high above the mountains you soar

Always searching for someone to feed,
Always giving a little more

Helping broken wings to heal

Ambassador

An Ambassador of Christ
A man who fears the Father not men
A man the Father holds in the palm of His hand
One who truly knows the Father's love
Always giving of himself
So others can truly know the Trinity

An Ambassador of Christ
Wearing the full armor of God
The armor worn confidently to protect and defend him
Satan’s plans can’t defeat those in the full armor of God

The belt of truth worn securely around his waist
Holding the truth, God’s word, firmly within
A man stands strong, honest and trustworthy
The belt fastened tightly ready for battle

The breastplate of righteousness placed upon his chest
To stand against injustices and corruption
Satan’s deception unable to touch
Though he fights for much
Living water flows out of a man
Keeping him whole and strong
Protected from all evil deception

The Gospel of Peace worn upon his
Feet for every step he takes
God's peace is felt around him
Faithfully representing God with every step
Such willing feet carrying His peace

Always moving forward with the shield of faith
Extinguishing the flaming darts of the enemy
Preventing any snare of temptation
Keeping his faith shining for all to see

The helmet of salvation clearly protecting his mind
Capturing every thought
Empowering him to defeat darkness
As the enemy's swipes fall harmlessly

The Sword of the Spirit, God's Word, cutting through all evil
For the power of his Sword has no restraint
Every word pierces the enemy
For the sword of the Spirit is sharper than any other
Bringing down evil with power of one blow

Clearly an Ambassador for Christ he is
Dressed in the full armor of God
Defeating the enemy and walking in the Victory

Made in the USA
Columbia, SC
06 March 2025

54608117R10072